Participant/Resource Guide

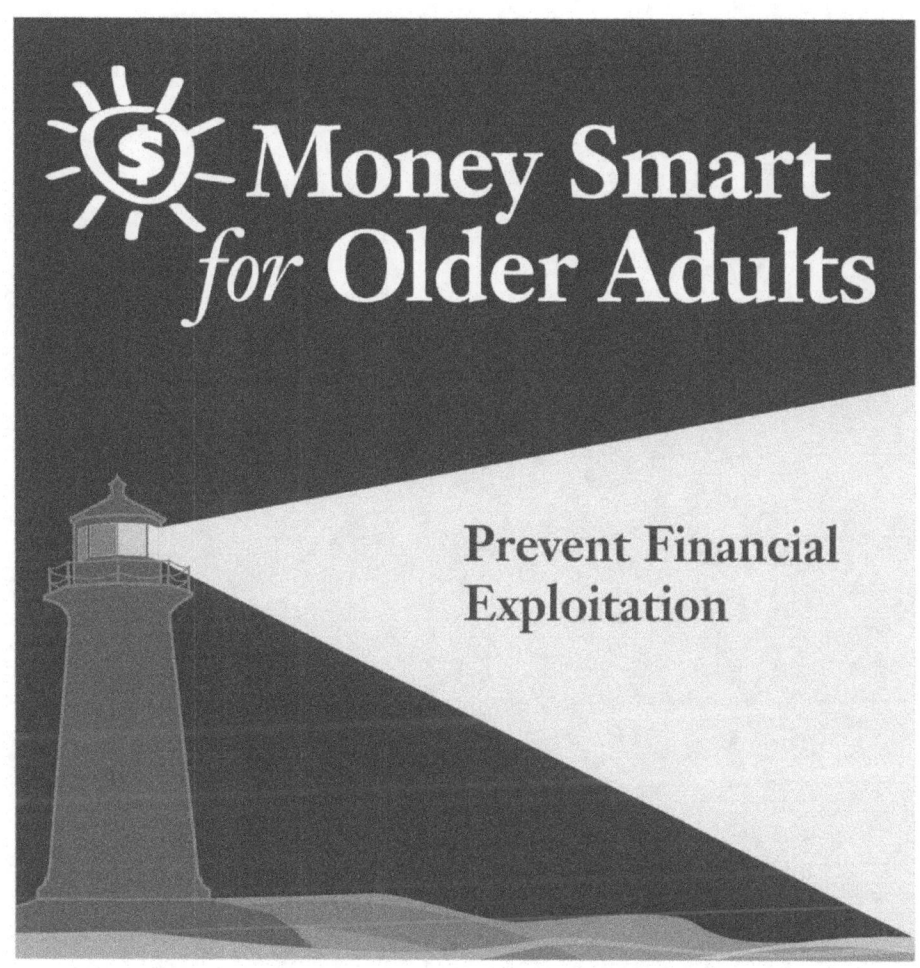

☀ $ Money Smart
for Older Adults

Prevent Financial
Exploitation

cfpb Consumer Financial
Protection Bureau

FDIC
FEDERAL DEPOSIT INSURANCE CORPORATION

Release Date: 06-2013

Welcome to Money Smart for Older Adults!

With over 50 million Americans aged 62 and older[1], Older Adults are prime targets for financial exploitation both by persons they know and trust and by strangers. Financial exploitation has been called "the crime of the 21st century" with one study suggesting that older Americans lost at least $2.9 billion to financial exploitation by a broad spectrum of perpetrators in 2010.[2]

A key factor in some cases of elder financial exploitation is mild cognitive impairment which can diminish an older adult's ability to make sound financial decisions.

This epidemic is under the radar. The cases tend to be very complex and can be difficult to investigate and prosecute. Elders who lose their life savings usually have little or no opportunity to regain what they have lost. Elder financial abuse can result in the loss of the ability to live independently; decline in health; broken trust, and fractured families.

Awareness and prevention is the first step. Planning ahead for financial wellbeing and the possibility of diminished financial capacity is critical. Reporting and early intervention that results in loss prevention is imperative.

Money Smart for Older Adults is designed to provide you with information and tips to help prevent common frauds, scams and other types of elder financial exploitation in your community. Please share this information as appropriate.

---

[1] 2010 Census: 57 million are 60 and over; 40 million aged 65 and over.
[2] *The MetLife Study of Elder Financial Abuse: Crimes of Occasion, Desperation, and Predation against America's Elders* (New York, NY: MetLife, June 2011).

Acknowledgements

The FDIC and CFPB wish to thank the following agencies for contributing to the information covered in this course:

- US Department of Health and Human Services' Administration for Community Living/Administration on Aging – Senior Medicare Patrol
- Federal Trade Commission
- Securities and Exchange Commission
- Social Security Administration
- Financial Industry Regulatory Authority, Inc.

Table of Contents

Checking In

Welcome

Welcome to *Money Smart for Older Adults*! By taking this course, you'll learn important points to consider in planning for a more secure financial future, including how to guard against identity theft and other forms of financial exploitation, how to prepare financially for unexpected life events, and what to have ready in case disaster strikes.

Objectives

After completing this module, you will be better able to:

- Recognize and reduce the risk of elder financial exploitation
- Guard against identity theft
- Plan for possible loss of your ability to manage your finances
- Prepare financially for disasters
- Find other helpful resources for managing your money and reporting financial exploitation

Participant Materials

The Participant/Resource Guide contains:

- Information and activities to help you learn the material
- Tools and instructions to complete the activities
- A glossary of the terms used in this module
- Resources for information on managing your money and reporting financial exploitation

Getting Started

Let's start by establishing an understanding of elder financial exploitation. Financial exploitation is a form of elder abuse. Elder abuse can take many forms, alone or in combination, including physical, psychological, emotional, or sexual abuse, neglect, abandonment, and self-neglect.

What is elder financial exploitation?

As defined by the Older Americans Act:

Financial exploitation is the fraudulent or otherwise illegal, unauthorized, or improper actions by a caregiver, fiduciary, or other individual in which the resources of an older person are used by another for personal profit or gain; or actions that result in depriving an older person of the benefits, resources, belongings, or assets to which they are entitled.

Elder financial exploitation is the theft of money, property or belongings.

Who is at risk for elder financial exploitation?

Anyone can be the victim of financial exploitation. Financial exploitation crosses all social, educational, and economic boundaries.

Why are older adults at risk of financial exploitation?

The following circumstances or conditions, especially in combination, can make an older adult more vulnerable to financial exploitation.

Older adults may:
- Have regular income and accumulated assets
- Be trusting and polite
- Be lonely and socially isolated
- Be vulnerable due to grief from the loss of a spouse, family member, friend, or pet
- Be reluctant to report exploitation by a family member, caregiver, or someone they depend on
- Be dependent on support from a family member or caregiver to remain independent
- Be receiving care from a person with substance abuse, gambling or financial problems, or mental health issues
- Fear retaliation by the exploiter

- Be unfamiliar with managing financial matters
- Be unprepared for retirement and the potential loss of financial decision-making capacity
- Have cognitive impairments that affect financial decision-making and judgment
- Be dependent on a family member, caregiver or another person who may pressure them for money or control of their finances.

What are some examples of financial exploitation?

- Exploitation by an agent under Power of Attorney or person in a fiduciary relationship (see glossary for definition of fiduciary)
- Theft of money or property, often by a caregiver or in-home helper
- Investment fraud and scams, including deceptive "free-lunch seminars" selling unnecessary or fraudulent financial services or products
- Lottery and sweepstakes scams
- Scams by telemarketers, mail offers or door-to-door salespersons
- Computer and Internet scams
- Identity theft
- Reverse mortgage fraud
- Contractor fraud and home improvement scams

Who are the abusers?

Perpetrators of financial exploitation can be:

- Family members and caregivers
- Friends, neighbors or acquaintances
- Persons with Power of Attorney or the legal authority to access or manage your money
- Telephone and mail scammers
- Financial advisers
- Internet scammers
- Home repair contractors
- Medicare scam operators
- Other persons known or unknown to the older adult

Why do you think older adults don't report financial exploitation?

- **Shame and embarrassment** – Many people are ashamed to admit that they have been financially exploited.
- **Loyalty** – Reluctance to report a family member, caregiver or other person who may treat them well in other ways.
- **Fear of retaliation**, not being believed or losing their independence by being declared incompetent and moved into a "nursing home."
- **Dependence** on the abuser for care or assistance.
- **Denial** – Some victims are unwilling or unable to acknowledge that financial exploitation is happening to them.
- **Self-blame** – Abuse can erode an older person's self-esteem, and some victims may believe they deserve or have caused the abuse.
- **Lack of awareness** – Some victims are unaware that they are being exploited, or don't know to whom they can report financial exploitation.

What should you do if you or someone you know becomes a victim of financial exploitation or another form of elder abuse?

In most cases, you would contact Adult Protective Services, generally a part of your county or state department of social services. You can find contact information at www.eldercare.gov, a public service provided by the U.S. Administration on Aging, or by calling 1-800-677-1116.

For cases of identity theft, contact your local police and the Federal Trade Commission (FTC). If the loss involves funds held in a financial institution, such as a bank or credit union, report the problem to the institution immediately.

If you have concerns with an FDIC-supervised financial institution, go to www2.fdic.gov/starsmail/index.asp

You will find more information at the end of this guide. Of course, if the person is in danger or you believe a crime has been committed, call 911 for immediate help.

Common Types of Older Adult Financial Exploitation

This module doesn't cover all types of elder financial exploitation in depth however it does discuss the key points and give some general guidelines you can use to help you identify fraud, scams and other types of financial exploitation and tips to help you prevent it from happening. This guide also provides a list of resources that you can consult as the need arises.

Power of Attorney (POA) or Fiduciary Abuse

A person who is named to manage your money or property is a fiduciary. He or she has a duty to manage your money and property for your benefit however he or she may abuse that power.

The person you appoint as your fiduciary should be trustworthy and honest. Your fiduciary can removed if they do not fulfill their obligations or duties. Fiduciaries can be sued and may be ordered to repay money. If elder financial exploitation is reported to the police or Adult Protective Service, the fiduciary could be investigated. If the fiduciary is convicted of stealing your assets, he or she can go to jail.

One way some older adults prepare for the possibility of diminished financial decision-making capacity is by making a power of attorney for finances and designating someone they trust to handle their financial decisions if they no longer can.

Creating a POA is a private way to appoint a substitute decision maker and is relatively inexpensive. If you don't appoint a POA before your decision-making ability declines, a family member or friend might have to go to court to have a guardian appointed – and that process can be lengthy, expensive, and very public.

A POA does involve some risk. It gives someone else – your agent – a great deal of authority over your finances without regular oversight. POA abuse can take many forms:
- Your agent might pressure you for authority that you do not want to grant.
- Your agent may spend your money on him or herself rather than for your benefit.
- Your agent might do things you didn't authorize him or her to do – for example, make gifts or change beneficiaries on insurance policies or retirement plans.

Different types of POAs

Some states allow for different types of POAs. Generally, a Power of Attorney goes into effect as soon as it is signed unless the document specifies a different arrangement. That means that even if you are capable of making decisions, your representative can immediately act on your behalf.

A "Durable" Power of Attorney remains effective even if the maker loses the capacity to make financial decisions.

There are different types of powers of attorney and ways to customize this document to fit your needs and preferences. Talk to an attorney for help in making a POA that is appropriate for your circumstances.

What are some ways to minimize the risk of POA abuse?

- Trust, but verify. Only appoint someone you really trust and make sure they know your wishes and preferences. You can require in your POA that your agent regularly report to another person on the financial transactions he or she makes on your behalf.
- Avoid appointing a person who has substance abuse, gambling problems, or who mismanages money.
- Tell friends, family members, and financial advisers about your POA so they can look out for you.
- Ask your bank about their POA procedures. The bank may have its own form you are required to complete (although a POA that is valid under your state's law should be accepted by financial service providers).
- Remember that POA designations are not written in stone – you can change them. If you decide that your agent isn't the best person to handle your finances, you can revoke (cancel) your POA. Notify your financial institution if you do this.
- Avoid appointing hired caregivers or other paid helpers as your agent under Power of Attorney.
- Beware of someone who wants to help you out by handling your finances and be your new "best friend." If an offer of help seems too good to be true, it probably is.

Plan ahead! A durable power of attorney is a very important tool in planning for financial incapacity due to Alzheimer's disease, another form of dementia, or other health problems. It is advisable to consult with an attorney when preparing a power of attorney, trust or any legal document giving someone else authority over your finances.

If you or a loved one is a victim of financial exploitation by a fiduciary, take action immediately and make a report to Adult Protective Services or your local law enforcement agency.

Abuse by Caregivers and In-Home Helpers

Family members and caregivers are common perpetrators of elder financial exploitation.

You can take steps to guard against financial exploitation if you or your loved one needs someone to help at home.

- Secure your valuables such as jewelry and other property.
- Secure your private financial documents including checks, financial statements and credit cards. ***Consider a locked file cabinet.***
- Require receipts for purchases made by helpers.
- Monitor bank accounts and telephone bills – Ask for help from a third party, if needed, and consider an automatic bill pay system. Consider setting up transaction alerts that are monitored by a family member or other third party.
- Do not let hired caregivers or helpers open your mail, pay your bills, or manage your finances.
- Never promise money or assets to someone when you die in exchange for care provided now.
- Never lend employees money or personal property.
- If you have trouble reading your statement, ask your bank if a second copy of your bank statement can go to someone who can read it for you. (Also, your bank may be able to send you your bank statement in large print.) This person does not need to have authority to act on your behalf.
- Never let caregivers use your credit/debit card to run errands or make purchases for you.

Investment Fraud

We've all heard the timeless saying "If it sounds too good to be true, it probably is." As an investor, these are good words to live by. The trick is knowing when "good" becomes "too good."

Senior certifications and designations

A popular practice among financial services salespeople is to identify themselves by a "senior designation" to signal that they have expertise in retirement or the investment needs of older people.

The requirements to earn and maintain a senior designation vary considerably. Programs of study range from weekend seminars to two-year graduate programs. The initials on a business card don't provide information about the quality of the designation. Some designations indicate extensive knowledge in senior financial needs, while others are merely marketing tools.

While the vast majority of investment advisers, financial planners, and broker-dealers are honest and reputable, it pays to check on a senior designation if you are presented with one. Be wary of investment scams, including the ones listed below.

Common investment scams

- **Ponzi schemes:** This is an old scam with a simple formula: Scammers promise high returns to investors. Money from new investors is used to pay previous investors. These schemes eventually collapse—leaving most of the investors with a financial loss.
- **Promissory notes:** A promissory note is a form of debt – similar to a loan or an IOU – that a company may issue to raise money. Typically, an investor agrees to loan money to the company for a set period of time. In exchange, the company promises to pay the investor a fixed return on his or her investment. While promissory notes can be legitimate investments, those that are marketed broadly to individual investors often turn out to be scams.
- **Unscrupulous financial advisers:** Some advisers cut corners or resort to outright fraud or bilking older adults with unexplained fees, unauthorized trades or other irregularities.

- **Affinity fraud:** Involves targeting persons with military, religious or spiritual affiliations, by ethnic identity, etc.
- **Internet fraud – the "Dot-Con:"** Internet fraud has become a booming business. With the growing number of older adults using the Internet, it is increasingly easy for con artists to reach millions of potential older victims at minimal cost.
- **Inappropriate or fraudulent annuity sales.** Variable annuities are often pitched to seniors through "free lunch" investment seminars. These products can be unsuitable for many retirees and are sometimes sold by salespersons who fail to disclose steep sales commissions and surrender charges that impose costly fees or penalties if you decide that you need your money before the maturity date.

How to check out your broker or investment adviser

You can check a broker's background via the Financial Industry Regulatory Authority (FINRA) BrokerCheck at www.finra.org , or by calling the FINRA BrokerCheck Hotline at 1-800 289-9999. You may also contact the state securities office and Better Business Bureau.

To learn more about senior certification and designations, visit FINRA at http://www.finra.org/industry/issues/seniors/p124734. Scroll to the bottom of the FINRA page to find links to other helpful resources.

Financial loss prevention tips

Invest wisely online and offline. Here are some important tips you should keep in mind when you are considering purchasing investment products and for protecting those investments once you have them:

- Never judge a person's trustworthiness by the sound of their voice.
- Take your time when making investment choices. Be careful of "act now" or "before it's too late" statements.
- Say "no" to anybody who tries to pressure you or rush you into an investment.
- Be wary of salespeople who prey upon your fears or promise returns that sound too good to be true.
- Always ask for a written explanation of any investment opportunity and then shop around and get a second opinion.
- Be wary of any financial adviser who tells you to leave everything in his or her care.

- Stay in charge of your money or enlist the help of a trusted third party to assist you.
- Make checks payable to a company or financial institution, never an individual.
- Retain and maintain account statements and confirmations you receive about your investment transaction.
- Document all conversations with financial advisers.
- Take immediate action if you detect a problem. Time is critical, so do not be afraid to complain.
- Don't let embarrassment or fear stop you from reporting financial exploitation or investment fraud.
- Don't put all your eggs in one basket— divide your investments among different asset categories, such as stocks, bonds, and cash held in federally insured deposit accounts

Here are additional tips to keep in mind when considering investment products

- Have enough emergency money in a savings or other readily accessible federally insured deposit account to support you and your family for at least six months before investing in non-deposit products.
- Do your homework. Never invest in a product you do not understand.
- Attend classes, seminars, or check the business reference section of the public library to become better informed.
- Be aware that many investment professionals offer "free seminars" as a marketing technique for obtaining new clients. Be sure to check the background of the presenter, research any recommended investment products, and get a second opinion before making the decision to invest.
- Understand the risks before investing. Investments always have some degree of risk.
- Be sure your financial adviser knows your financial objectives and risk tolerance.

Understanding FDIC insurance

If you select investment products offered by a bank, it is important to understand which of your investments are covered by the Federal Deposit Insurance Corporation or FDIC. The FDIC insures funds in deposit accounts at FDIC-insured institutions including:

- Checking
- Savings

- Money Market Deposit Accounts (MMDAs)
- Certificates of Deposit (CDs)

Another federal agency, the National Credit Union Administration, provides similar deposit insurance coverage to depositors at federally insured credit unions.

FDIC insurance protects depositors up to a capped amount in the event of a bank failure. It does **not** protect depositors from losses resulting from theft, fraud, or robbery.

FDIC insurance also does not cover other financial products and services that insured banks may offer (e.g., stocks, bonds, mutual fund shares, life insurance policies, annuities and municipal securities). These products should be sold separately by individuals who do not offer insured deposit products. Be alert when bank personnel transfer you to another "representative." **Read the disclosures carefully. Disclosures for non-deposit products must indicate that they are NOT FDIC insured.**

By law, federal deposit insurance is backed by the full faith and credit of the Federal Government. If a bank fails, the FDIC will pay all insured deposits up to the insurance limit, including principal and any accrued interest through the date of the bank closing. Federal law requires that all insured deposits be paid as soon as possible.

Insurance coverage and ownership categories

Deposit insurance coverage is based on a depositor's ability to meet the specific requirements for an ownership category. The most common account ownership categories for individual and family deposits are single accounts, joint accounts, revocable trust accounts, and certain retirement accounts.

Each ownership category has different requirements, and the potential amount of insurance coverage for each category is based on the Standard Maximum Deposit Insurance Amount (SMDIA), which is $250,000.

For additional details on the coverage limits, requirements, and in-depth information on all account ownership categories and other types of deposit accounts, visit www.fdic.gov/deposit/deposits, call toll-free **1-877-ASK-FDIC (1-877-275-3342)**, or talk to your bank representative.

Lottery and Sweepstakes Scams

Sweepstakes scams may come in the form of a telephone call or an email that congratulates the recipient on winning a lottery, drawing, or sweepstakes that they usually have not even entered. The scammer asks the "winner" for an upfront payment, perhaps to cover a processing fee or taxes. Another variation of this scam involves a letter, sometimes with an authentic looking "Claim Certificate" or a "check" as an advance to pay the winnings. Although bankers are generally aware of this scam and how to spot the phony checks, if deposited, the financial institution may hold the victim responsible for repayment of the entire amount of the fraudulent check and the overdraft charges that may result.

Sweepstakes Recovery Scam

Once it is apparent that no winnings are forthcoming, the victim may receive another call from a person claiming to be an attorney representing sweepstakes winners. In exchange for an upfront fee, the so-called attorney offers to collect the winnings on behalf of the victim. Needless to say, the "attorney" is actually an associate of the original scammer.

Telephone Scams

Older adults are increasingly the targets of scam artists on the telephone who use lies, deception, and fear tactics to convince the elder to send them money or provide personal account information. An example of a common scam Money Smart for Older Adults explores is the "grandparent scam ." In this scam, an imposter calls a grandparent pretending to be a grandchild in trouble; the scammer may even know the grandchild's name. The scammer is usually crying making it hard to recognize the grandchild's voice. The scammer pleads for the grandparent to immediately wire money and not tell any family members for fear of upsetting them. Many people will immediately jump to the assistance of the grandchild and won't ask questions until later. They also know that many older people will have experienced a hearing loss and won't detect any differences from their grandchild's voice. Or they may attribute the differences they do hear to the stress of the situation.

Tips for Avoiding Telephone Scams

Scammers can be very convincing. If something seems unusual, check it out.

- Never "pay to play." A legitimate sweepstakes will not ask for money upfront.

- You cannot win a sweepstakes or lottery that you did not enter.

- Be suspicious of any pressure to send funds via wire transfer or a pre-paid reloadable card.

- Pay attention to warnings from your financial institution that a request sounds like a scam. Your banker may have encountered similar situations in the past.

- Scammers often claim an emergency, hoping you will take quick action without checking out the situation. Before offering help to a grandchild (or another relative or friend), be sure to telephone your grandchild or the parents at a number you know to be valid to find out if the request is legitimate.

- If a caller claims to be from an established organization such as a hospital or law enforcement agency, look up the number of the organization independently before taking action.

- Consider it a red flag if the caller insists on secrecy. Never allow anyone to isolate or discourage you from seeking information, verification, support and counsel from family members, friends or trusted advisors prior to making any financial transaction.

Activity 1: Telephone Scams

Read each scenario and then, based on what you have learned, answer the questions in the space provided:

Scenario 1

Myra is home watching TV when the telephone rings. She answers the call and the man on the line says "Congratulations! You've won $2.7 million dollars in the lottery!" Myra is surprised. Although she buys lottery tickets, she hasn't given her name to anyone. The caller tells her that there are a couple of things she needs to do to complete the process so she can receive her check. He directs Myra to go to her bank and withdraw $2,700 to cover processing fees. He tells her to forward the funds through a local wire service or to buy and send a special prepaid card that she can get to expedite the process. Myra heads to her bank to withdraw the money. The next day the person calls to say they received the funds and an additional $5,000 is needed to pay the taxes.

What are the red flags that should warn Myra that she is about to become a victim of a scam?

_____

_____

_____

_____

Scenario 2

A few weeks after Myra used a pre-paid card to transfer money to the scammer, she received a call from a person claiming to be an attorney representing sweepstakes winners. The attorney offered to collect the winnings for Myra but she would have to pay his $7,000 fee up front.

What should Myra do?

_____

_____

_____

_____

Scenario 3

Jack lives alone in his home of 40 years. He has become increasingly hard of hearing, which has made it difficult for him to communicate on the telephone. One afternoon he receives a call from a distressed-sounding person who says "Hi Grandpa, this is your favorite grandson." When Jack asks "is this Johnny?" the caller says "yes grandpa, it's Johnny." Johnny says he's in Canada and has been arrested. Johnny explains that he needs Jack to wire $2,500 to bail him out. Johnny also says "please don't tell mom – I don't want her to be upset." Jack hurries to his bank or credit union and insists on wiring the money despite warnings from the teller and the bank manager that this sounds like a scam.

What are the red flags in this story?

_____

_____

_____

_____

Computer/Internet Scams

Lack of familiarity with internet security and scams such as **phishing** and **spoofing** can dupe older adults into giving out personal financial information. Phishing scammers create authentic-looking emails, text messages, and Internet pages to entice their victims to disclose financial information such as credit card details, bank or credit card account numbers, Social Security numbers, etc.

Here are some examples:

- "We suspect an unauthorized transaction on your account. To ensure that your account is not compromised, please click the link below and confirm your identity."
- "During our regular verification of accounts, we couldn't verify your information. Please click here to update and verify your information."
- "Our records indicate that your account was overcharged. You must call us within 7 days to receive your refund."

The messages may appear to be from organizations you do business with–such as your financial institution. They may threaten to close your account or take other action if you don't respond.

The senders are "phishing" for your private account information so they can use it to commit fraud or identity theft against you.

Spoofing scammers disguise an email address to look like it is coming from someone else. For example, you may receive an email that looks like it is coming from a friend who needs immediate funds to cope with an emergency.

Tips for avoiding computer or Internet scams

Take precautions with your personal computer (PC) to reduce your risk of a computer/Internet attack:

- Use trusted security software and make sure it's updated frequently.
- Do not email financial information or account numbers. Email is not a secure method of transmitting personal information.
- Be cautious about opening attachments and downloading files from emails, regardless of who sent them. These files can contain viruses or other malware that can compromise your computer's security.
- Use passwords that will be hard for hackers to guess. For example, use a mix of numbers, symbols, and letters instead of easily guessed words.
- Shut down your PC when you are not using it.

For practical tips to help you guard against Internet fraud, secure your computer, and protect your personal information, visit www.OnGuardOnline.gov.

How to Respond to a Phishing [or Spoofing] Attack

Even if you use security software, chances are that some questionable messages will get through. Some of these messages look very realistic. Here are some tips for protecting yourself.

- Do not open any message that comes from an unfamiliar source. If you open a suspicious message, delete it. Do not click on links or call telephone numbers provided in the message. Be wary about opening attachments.

- Delete email and text messages that ask you to confirm or provide personal information (credit card and bank account numbers, Social Security numbers, passwords, etc.). Legitimate companies never ask for this information via email or text.
- If you're concerned about your account or need to reach an organization that you do business with, call the number on your financial statements or on the back of your credit card or in the telephone book. Do not call the telephone number that the caller or spoof website provides you!
- If you receive an email that looks like it is from a friend or relative asking you to send money, call to verify that the email really came from them.

For more information, go to http://onguardonline.gov/articles/0003-phishing.
Victims of phishing could become victims of identity theft. If you might have been tricked by a phishing email, act promptly to avoid financial loss or damage to your credit. You'll find more information at the end of the following section on Identity Theft.

Identity Theft

Identity theft occurs when thieves steal your personal information (e.g., your Social Security number (SSN), birth date, credit card numbers, personal identification numbers (PINs), or passwords). With sufficient information, another person can become you and use your identity to commit fraud or other crimes.

How to Avoid Identity Theft

- **Protect your SSN, credit card and debit card numbers, PINs, passwords, and other personal information.**
  Never provide this information in response to an unwanted telephone call, fax, letter, or email, no matter how friendly or official the circumstances may appear. Be mindful of those who may be "shoulder surfing" (or trying to look over your shoulder) while you use the ATM, and seeking to steal your PIN. In case your wallet is lost or stolen, carry only the identification you really need: checks, credit cards, or debit cards. Keep the rest, including your Social Security card, in a safe place. Do not preprint your SSN, telephone number, or driver's license number on your checks. You do not have to give merchants

your Social Security number. Ask the merchant to use another form of identification that does not include your SSN (e.g., a passport).

- **Protect your incoming and outgoing mail.**

  For incoming mail: Try to use a locked mailbox or other secure location (e.g., a post office box). If your mailbox is not locked or in a secure location, try to promptly remove mail that has been delivered or move the mailbox to a safer place. When ordering new checks, ask about having the checks delivered to your bank branch instead of having them mailed to your home where you run the risk of a thief finding them outside your front door.

  For outgoing mail containing a check or personal information: Try to deposit it in a United States (U.S.) Postal Service blue collection box, hand it to a mail carrier, or take it to the post office instead of leaving it in your doorway or home mailbox. A mailbox that holds your outgoing bills is a prime target for thieves who cruise neighborhoods looking for account information. Avoid putting up the flag on a mailbox to indicate that outgoing mail is waiting.

- **Sign up for direct deposit.**

  Sign up for direct deposit of your paycheck, retirement check, or state or federal benefits, (e.g., Social Security). Direct deposit prevents someone from stealing a check out of your mailbox and forging your signature to access your money. Direct deposit is also beneficial in the event of a disaster.

- **Keep your financial trash "clean."**

  Thieves known as dumpster divers pick through garbage looking for pieces of paper containing SSNs, bank account information, and other details they can use to commit fraud. What is your best protection against dumpster divers? Before tossing out these items, destroy them, preferably using a crosscut shredder that turns paper into confetti that cannot be easily reconstructed.

- **Keep a close watch on your bank account statements and credit card bills.**
  Monitor these statements each month and contact your financial institution immediately if there is a discrepancy in your records or if you notice something suspicious (e.g., a missing payment or an unauthorized withdrawal). Contact your institution if a bank statement or credit card bill does not arrive on time. Missing financially related mail could be a sign someone has stolen your mail and/or account information, and may have changed your mailing address to run up bills in your name from another location.

- **Avoid identity theft on the Internet.**
  As we mentioned in the section on Computer/Internet Scams, never provide bank account or other personal information in response to an unsolicited email, or when visiting a website that does not explain how personal information will be protected. Legitimate organizations would not ask you for these details because they already have the necessary information, or can obtain it in other ways. If you believe the email is fraudulent, consider bringing it to the attention of the Federal Trade Commission (FTC) via its online complaint form: www.ftccomplaintassistant.gov.

  If you do open and respond to a phony email, contact your financial institution immediately and follow the steps listed in the FTC brochures listed at the end of this guide. For more about avoiding phishing scams, visit http://onguardonline.gov/articles/0003-phishing.

- **Review your credit report annually and report fraudulent activity.**
  Review your credit report carefully for warning signs of actual or potential identity theft. For example, items that include mention of a credit card, loan, or lease you never signed up for, and requests for a copy of your credit report from someone you do not recognize could be a sign that a con artist is snooping around for personal information. To obtain a free copy of your credit report, visit www.annualcreditreport.com

Fraud Alert: Social Security Administration

The Inspector General for the Social Security Administration (SSA) is warning the public, and Social Security beneficiaries in particular, to be aware of fraud scams that target personal information.

In the most recent scam, identity thieves obtain the personal information of Social Security beneficiaries and use that information to attempt to open a 'my Social Security' account on SSA's website. If successful, they then use that account to redirect the beneficiary's direct deposit benefits to an account controlled by the thief.

This should in no way discourage people from using SSA's 'my Social Security' feature, which enables the public to view their earnings history and estimated benefits, and allows beneficiaries to obtain a host of services online; in fact establishing your account eliminates the risk of a new account being opened by an identity thief. This type of crime does, however, serve as a reminder to protect your personal information as you would any other thing of value. Once thieves have your personal information, they can use it to open credit accounts, buy homes, claim tax refunds, and commit other types of fraud.

If you receive information from SSA indicating that you have opened a 'my Social Security' account, and you did not open an account, you should contact Social Security so that appropriate action may be taken, and the matter may be referred to the Office of the Inspector General. You can do so by visiting or calling a local SSA office or calling SSA's toll free customer service at 1-800-772-1213. Deaf or hearing-impaired individuals can call Social Security's TTY number at 1-800-325-0778.

Get more information on identity theft

Visit the FTC's Identity Theft website at www.ftc.gov/idtheft for information on how to minimize your risk or call them at1-877-IDTHEFT (438-4338).

Identity Theft: If You Think You May Be a Victim

If you believe you are a victim of identity theft, the FTC recommends that you immediately take the following actions:

- Place an initial fraud alert with one of the three nationwide credit reporting companies
- Order your credit reports
- Create an identity theft report
- Consider placing an extended fraud alert or security freeze on your credit report to limit the circumstances under which a credit reporting company may release your credit report.

For more information:

http://www.consumer.ftc.gov/articles/0279-extended-fraud-alerts-and-credit-freezes

The FTC has many resources available to help you. Call the FTC's Identity Theft Hotline at 1-877-IDTHEFT (438-4338) or visit www.ftc.gov/idtheft . Its online toolkit includes:

- A brochure covering the basics –*Identity Theft: What To Know, What To Do*
- A detailed guide for protecting your information, with instructions and sample letters to help identity theft victims–*Taking Charge: What to Do If Your Identity Is Stolen* Sample letters to help you dispute unauthorized charges or the opening of new accounts in your name. Sample letters and forms are available at http://www.consumer.ftc.gov/articles/0281-sample-letters-and-forms-victims-identity-theft

Medical Identity Theft

Medical identity theft is serious business. According to one study, about 1.5 million adults are victims of medical identity theft each year.

What Is Medical Identity Theft?

Medical ID theft occurs when someone steals personal information — such as your name and Medicare number — and uses the information to get medical treatment, prescription drugs, surgery or other services and then bills Medicare for it. Medicare ID theft is a form of Medicare fraud.

A thief may use your name or health insurance numbers to see a doctor, get prescription drugs, file claims with your insurance provider, or get other care. If the thief's health information is mixed with yours, your treatment, insurance and payment records, and credit report may be affected.

If you see signs of medical identity theft, order copies of your records and check for mistakes. You have the right to see your records and have mistakes corrected.

Medical ID theft can cause financial harm but it is about more than losing time and money. Sometimes people are denied a Medicare service or equipment because their records falsely show they already received it, when in fact it went to someone posing as them.

It can affect your medical and health insurance records. Every time a thief uses your identity to get care, a record is created with incorrect medical information about you. That information might include:
- A different blood type
- An inaccurate history of drug or alcohol abuse
- Test results that are not yours
- A diagnosis of an illness, allergy or condition that you do not have

Any of these could lead to you receiving the wrong treatment and even being injured or getting sick due to an incorrect treatment.

All types of people, including doctors and medical equipment companies, have been caught stealing people's medical identities. There have even been links to the mafia and thieves in other countries. Sadly, about one-third of medical identity thieves are family members.

How Do You Learn if You Are a Victim?

Here are some warning signs that your identity may be stolen:
- You get a bill for medical services you did not receive.
- You are contacted by a debt collection company for money you do not owe.
- Your insurance company says you've reached your limit on medical benefits.
- You are denied insurance for a medical condition you do not have.

How to Avoid Medical Identity Theft

- Protect your Medicare and other health insurance cards in the same way you would protect a credit card.
- Review your Medicare Summary Notices (MSN), Explanations of Benefits (EOB) statements and medical bills for suspicious charges. If you find incorrect information in your records, insist that it be corrected or removed.
- Only give personal information to Medicare-approved doctors, other providers and suppliers; your State Health Insurance Assistance Program or Senior Medicare Patrol (SMP) program; or Social Security. [Call 1-800-MEDICARE (1-800-633-4227) if you aren't sure if a provider is approved by Medicare.]
- Beware of offers of free medical equipment, services or goods in exchange for your Medicare number.
- Shred papers with your medical identity before putting them in the trash. Remove or destroy labels on prescription bottles and packages before you put them in the trash.

How to Respond if You Suspect Medical Identity Theft

- Ask your health care provider for a copy of your current medical file. If anything seems wrong, write to your health plan or provider and ask for a correction.
- Contact your local Senior Medicare Patrol (see contact information below.)

How Your Senior Medicare Patrol (SMP) Can Help

Your local SMP is ready to provide you with the information you need to protect yourself from Medicare errors, fraud and abuse, detect potential errors, and report your concerns.

For more information or to locate your state SMP, visit www.smpresource.org

Activity 2: Identity Theft Self-Check

Review each response on the list and indicate whether you perform this action always, sometimes, or never. Then, tally your score and see how well you are taking measures to avoid identity theft.

	Always (2 points)	Sometimes (1 point)	Never (0 points)
1. Cover or block the Point of Service (POS)/ATM keypad when I enter my PIN			
2. Carry only the identification, checks, credit cards, or debit cards I really need			
3. Use direct deposit for paychecks, tax refunds, benefits payments, etc.			
4. Shred documents with personal/financial information before disposing of/recycling them			
5. Use complex passwords with a mix of numbers, symbols, and letters instead of easily guessed words			
6. Review financial statements/bills monthly and identify/correct errors			
7. Review my credit report annually and identify/correct errors			
8. Use secure mailboxes for incoming/outgoing mail			
9. Avoid providing/sharing personal information (e.g., SSN) whenever possible			
10. Review my Medicare Summary Notices (MSN), Explanations of Benefits (EOB) statements and medical bills for suspicious charges.			
Total each column			
Grand Total			

Scores:

0–6: You are not taking many actions to minimize your risk of identity theft. Consider what you have learned today, and consider how you can implement steps to protect your identity.

7–13: You have developed some good practices to avoid identity theft; however, you have room for improvement. Consider what actions you need to take or apply more regularly to better protect your identity.

14–20: You are doing a great job at minimizing your risk of identity theft. Continue to apply these actions regularly and determine what additional steps you can take to protect your identity.

Planning For Unexpected Life Events

Planning ahead:

- Gives you control; you make choices for your situation
- Relieves the stress of decision-making from caretakers/family members
- Saves money and helps you avoid financial disaster or setback
- Allows time for gathering information, comparing options, and determining which options help achieve what is most important

Preparing for possible future health problems

The majority of people who need long-term care are older adults. However, the need for long-term care can come at any age due to disabling diseases, car accidents, brain injuries, strokes, and other disabling events.

Families and individuals who plan ahead before a disability will be in a better position to cope in the event of a disability. Consider taking these steps before you or a family member becomes ill or disabled:

- **Prepare a plan.** Start with reviewing your income and expenses.
- **Make sure trusted family members know where to find personal and financial documents in an emergency.**
- **Set up direct deposit for income and benefit checks.** Direct deposit delivers your Social Security or Supplemental Security Income (SSI) benefit or other income sources into your bank, savings and loan, or credit union account quickly and safely.
- **Consider automatic payment** of important, recurring bills.
- **Consider a durable power of attorney.** As we mentioned in the section on Power of Attorney, this legal document gives one or more people the authority to handle finances and remains in effect if you become incapacitated.
- **Make sure you are properly insured.** Speak with a financial planner or an insurance agent you trust. Review your policy regulary because your needs can change.
- **Maintain a healthy lifestyle.**

Experts also recommend a health care power of attorney or health care proxy designating a family member or other trusted person to make decisions about medical treatment. Living wills and health care proxies are intended to ensure that someone's wishes regarding medical care are honored.

Direct Deposit of your Social Security Benefit

Let's go into a little more detail about direct deposit of your Social Security and Supplemental Security Income (SSI) benefit payments. Applicants filing for these benefits must now choose either direct deposit or the Direct Express® debit card. Currently entitled beneficiaries and recipients who had been receiving payment by check have had to switch to direct deposit to a checking account or a pre-paid card they select or to the Direct Express® debit card.

How direct deposit of your Social Security benefit works

The U.S. Treasury sends an electronic message to your bank, savings and loan, or credit union crediting your account with the exact amount of your Social Security or SSI benefit. You can withdraw money, put some in savings or pay bills–the ordinary things you do with your money. The difference is, your check isn't printed or mailed. For more information, please visit the Department of the Treasury's Go Direct® website http://www.godirect.org

How to Be Financially Prepared for Disasters

Natural or man-made disasters can strike without warning and can happen anywhere. These include floods, fires, earthquakes, tornadoes, hurricanes, chemical spills or similar events that can force people to evacuate their homes. Even minor disasters can damage or destroy property or other belongings. They can also seriously impair your ability to conduct essential financial transactions for a period of time. In addition to planning for your personal safety and basic needs (e.g., shelter, food, and water), you should be ready to deal with financial challenges, including how to pay for supplies or temporary housing if necessary.

What to Have Ready

Consider keeping the following documents, bank products, and other items in a secure place and readily available in an emergency:

- **Forms of identification:** These primarily include driver's licenses (or state identification cards for non-drivers), insurance cards, Social Security card, passport, and birth certificate.
- **Your checkbook with enough blank checks and deposit slips to last at least a month**
- **ATM cards, debit cards (for use at ATMs and merchants), and credit cards:** Do not assume that merchants and ATMs in areas affected by a disaster will immediately be functioning as usual. Have other options available for getting cash and making payments.
- **Cash**
- **Telephone numbers for your financial services providers:** These include local and toll-free numbers for your bank, credit card companies, brokerage firms (for stocks, bonds, or mutual fund investments) and insurance companies.
- **Important account numbers:** These include bank and brokerage account numbers, credit card numbers, and homeowner's or renter's insurance policy numbers. You may want to copy the front and back of your credit cards (and keep them in a safe place).
- **The key to your safe deposit box**

What to Keep and Where to Keep It

After you have gathered your most important financial items and documents, protect them as well as you can while also ensuring you have access to them in an emergency. Here is a reasonable strategy for many people:

- Make backup copies of important documents.
- Make an electronic image of your documents so you can more easily store the information.
- Give a copy of your documents to loved ones or let them know where to find the documents in an emergency.
- Store your backups some distance from your home in case the disaster impacts your entire community.
- Make a record of all credit/debit cards with the account and contact numbers to report lost/stolen cards.

Determine what to keep at home and what to store in a safe deposit box at your bank.

A safe deposit box is best for protecting items of value and certain papers that could be difficult or impossible to replace, but not anything you might need to access quickly. What should you put in a safe deposit box? Examples include a birth certificate and originals of important contracts. What is better left safely at home, preferably in a durable, fireproof safe? Your passport and medical care directives because you might need these on short notice. Consult your attorney before putting an original will in a safe deposit box. Some states do not permit immediate access to a safe deposit box after a person dies, so there may be complications accessing a will stored in a safe deposit box. Remember that safe deposit boxes are not necessarily fireproof or waterproof.

Seal important documents in airtight and waterproof plastic bags or containers to prevent water damage.

Prepare one or more emergency evacuation bags.

Pack essential financial items and documents (e.g., cash, checks, copies of your credit cards and identification cards, a key to your safe deposit box, and contact information for your financial services providers). Make sure each evacuation bag is waterproof and easy to carry and kept in a secure place in your home. Periodically update the contents of the bag. It will not do you any good if the checks in your bag are for a closed account.

What Else to Consider

- **Arrange for automatic bill payments from your bank account.** This service enables you to make scheduled payments (e.g., for your telephone bill, insurance premiums and loan payments), and avoids late charges or service interruptions.
- **Sign up for Internet banking services.** This also makes it possible to conduct your banking business without writing checks. Only do this if you feel comfortable with keeping your internet security software up-to-date.
- **Review your insurance coverage.** Make sure you have enough insurance, including: personal property coverage, as applicable, to cover the cost to replace or repair your home, car and other valuable property.

To learn more about being financially prepared for disasters, visit www.fdic.gov/consumers/consumer/news/index.html and type *disaster preparedness* in the search box.

Activity 3: How Financially Prepared Are You?

Think about what you have learned today. In the space provided, jot down what documents you will gather and where you will put them.

_____
_____
_____
_____
_____
_____

Scams that Target Homeowners

Reverse Mortgage Proceeds Fraud
Scenario

To pay for his recommended home improvements, a handyman convinces an older woman to appoint him as her Power of Attorney so he can help her get a reverse mortgage on the home she had purchased in the 1950's and owns outright. When the lender provided a lump-sum payout, she never saw any of the money because the handyman used it for drugs, among other things.

What is a reverse mortgage?

Although Reverse Mortgages can be legitimate products and are appropriate for many consumers, scammers also sell these products to the disadvantage of their victims.

A reverse mortgage is a special type of loan that allows homeowners age 62 and older to borrow against the equity in their homes. It is called a "reverse" mortgage because you receive money from the lender, instead of making payments. The money you receive, and the interest charged on the loan, increases the balance of your loan each month. Over time, the equity you have in your home decreases as the amount you owe increases.

When you take out a reverse mortgage loan, you can receive your money as a line of credit available when you need it, in regular monthly installments, or up-front as a lump sum. You do not have to pay back the loan as long as you continue to live in the home, maintain your home, and stay current on expenses such as homeowner's insurance and property taxes. If you move out or die, the loan becomes due and must be paid off.

How borrowers get scammed

Scammers can take advantage of the fact that borrowers can receive the loan in the form of a lump sum payout. The reverse mortgage proceeds scam may include one or several of the following elements:

- Family members or others who pressure the older adult to get a reverse mortgage and then "borrow" the money or scam the elder out of the proceeds.
- Scammers who "require" an older borrower to sign a Power of Attorney or to sign proceeds over to a "loan officer or other agent" for future "disbursals." The scammers then embezzle a portion or all of the funds.
- Brokers who pressure or fraudulently require the borrower to purchase annuities, long-term care insurance, high risk investments or other financial products with the proceeds from the reverse mortgage in order to generate additional commissions.

Mortgage Assistance Rescue Scam

Beware of anyone who promises you can stay in your home or who asks for a lot of money to help you. Scammers might promise guaranteed or immediate relief from foreclosure, and they might charge you very high fees for little or no services.

Mortgage relief companies may not collect any fees until they have provided you with a written offer from a lender or servicer that you decide is acceptable and a written document from the lender or servicer describing the key changes to the mortgage that would result if you accept the offer. The companies also must remind you of your right to reject the offer without any charge.

Don't get scammed. There is help available at little or no cost to you. Foreclosure prevention counseling is available free of charge through HUD's Housing Counseling Program. Call the CFPB at 1-855-411-CFPB (2372) to be connected to a HUD-approved housing counselor.

Contractor Fraud and Home Improvement Scams

Scenario

Monica is 76 years old and lives alone in her home. One morning she is outside watering her garden when a truck pulls up and a man approaches her. He tells her that he is a building contractor and that he can see that she has a problem with her roof. He points to a spot near the chimney and tells her he can fix the problem now with the materials he has left over from a job he just finished nearby. He says he'll give her a big discount if she'll pay him today in cash. After going up on the roof and tearing off some roof tiles, he tells her that the problem is worse than he thought, but he can do it for $2,800. When Monica says she doesn't have $2,800 in cash, the contractor becomes angry and threatening. He says if Monica doesn't have the money she will have to take out a loan to pay him.

Contractor Fraud

Home Repair / Home Improvement Scams

Sooner or later every home needs repairs or improvements. Although some home improvement companies do good work, some may not provide the level of service you expect. Many homeowners are targeted by scam artists who use high pressure tactics to sell unneeded and overpriced contracts for "home improvements." Often these scam artists charge more than their quoted prices or their work does not live up to their promises. When the homeowner refuses to pay for shoddy or incomplete work, the contractor or an affiliated lender threatens foreclosure on the home.

Impersonating Officials

Con artists may pose as building inspectors and order immediate repairs which they can do on the side. They may also pose as government officials and demand a fee for processing emergency loan documents.

Tips for Avoiding Contractor Fraud

Here are some common sense tips to protect yourself from contractor fraud.

- Ask to see identification for anyone representing him or herself as a government official. Call the government agency to verify the identity if there is any payment of money involved.

- Get bids from several local, established contractors. Obtain at least three legible bids in writing and don't sign anything before carefully reading it. Do not do business with anyone who approaches you door-to-door or on the phone. Note that many states and local jurisdictions have laws regulating door-to-door sales.

- Avoid contractors who:
    - Are working door-to-door
    - Come from out of state
    - Don't provide an address and telephone number, or refuse to show identification

- Before beginning any home repair project, ask if the contractor has the required licenses (note license numbers) and is bonded. Seek out references from neighbors or members of your affinity groups (e.g., place of worship).

- Check with your state licensing agency's website or hotline to make sure the licenses are valid. Ask the licensing agencies if the contractor has a history of complaints.

- Get several references from previous customers. If possible, visit them to see the work done.

- Require the contractor you choose to provide you with a contract that contains clearly written payment terms.

- Don't pay in advance.

- Never pay with cash.

- Don't provide personal financial information, such as your checking account, credit card or debit card numbers.

- If you need to borrow money to pay for repairs, don't let the contractor steer you toward a particular lender.

- Do not make a final payment until you are satisfied with the job, all debris is removed from your property, and any necessary building inspections have been completed. If a contractor shows up at your door and pressures you to go to the bank with him to get cash to pay for a job you do not want done, if you ask to speak with the branch manager, the manager can call the police for you, who can show up at the branch. Being in public place with video cameras and witnesses should reduce your risk.

To get more information on home improvement, including: how to hire contractors, how to understand your payment options, and how to protect against home improvement scams, read the FTC brochure titled *Home Sweet Home Improvement.* The brochure is available at www.ftc.gov. Enter *home improvement* in the search field. You can also call the FTC to request the brochure at 1-877-FTC-HELP (382-4357).

Scams that Target Veterans Benefits

Pension Benefits Filing Scam

The Veterans Affairs' (VA) pension program provides monthly benefit payments to certain wartime veterans with financial need, and their survivors. Recipients also may be eligible for one of two additional amounts:

- Aid and Attendance (A&A) may be paid to veterans, or their surviving spouses, who require assistance with activities of daily living, are bedridden, are patients in nursing homes, or have a qualifying major vision loss.
- Housebound amounts may be paid to veterans or surviving spouses who are substantially confined to their homes because of a permanent disability.

Tips for avoiding VA pension benefits filing scams

- Be aware that an individual generally must be accredited by VA to assist you in preparing and filing a claim. To find an accredited attorney, claims agent, or veterans service organization (VSO), visit VA's Accreditation Search page at http://www.va.gov/ogc/apps/accreditation/index.asp
- Never pay a fee to anyone for preparing and filing your initial claim. Although an attorney may charge a consulting fee for advising you about the benefits for which you may be eligible, the clock stops running as soon as you indicate your intention to file.
- Avoid attorneys or claims agents who try to market financial products, such as trusts and annuities, in connection with filing your VA claim. Older veterans may face

problems with annuities since you may not have access to your funds, should you need them, without paying a costly surrender fee.

- Know that shifting your assets into certain types of investments in order to meet eligibility thresholds for VA pension benefits could make you ineligible for Medicaid for a period of time.

Lump-Sum Payment for Future Benefits Scam

Another scam targets veterans who receive either monthly disability compensation or pension payments. The scammer may offer a lump sum payment in exchange for the veteran's future benefits. Although Federal law prohibits assigning benefits to a third party, many scammers -- who usually identify themselves as corporate entities -- get around this limitation by representing the lump sum payment as an advance. Whatever the name, these transactions generally are not a good deal for the veteran.

Consider this example:

A veteran received a lump-sum payment of $73,000 in exchange for his monthly benefits check of $2,744 for a ten-year period. At the end of the ten years, the veteran's total repayment is estimated as $256,293. This translates to an annual interest rate of 44.5 percent.

Tips for avoiding the lump-sum payment scam

- Be aware that lump sum payment arrangements are very costly, often the equivalent of a 60 to 70 percent annual interest rate.
- Say no to arrangements that allow a creditor to access the account where you receive your benefits. Past arrangements have included joint checking accounts from which the scammer could withdraw funds as soon as they were deposited and accounts that remained in the veteran's name but that allowed the lump-sum provider to make monthly withdrawals in the amount of the benefit.
- Remember that your military benefits cannot be garnished by a creditor. Some lump-sum providers know this, of course, and may ask for additional collateral.
- Seek advice from a trusted financial expert if you need emergency funds. Other arrangements are less costly.

Where to Get More Information or Assistance

For help understanding your VA benefits, visit www.va.gov or call 1-800-827-1000. Also, the Federal Trade Commission:

http://www.ftc.gov/opa/2013/02/vetspension.shtm

Post-Test

Now that you have gone through the course, see what you have learned.

1. **Which of the following may be perpetrators of elder financial exploitation? Select all that apply.**
    a. Family members and caregivers
    b. Friends or neighbors
    c. Telephone and mail scammers
    d. Financial advisers

2. **What is true of a durable power of attorney (POA)? Select all that apply.**
    a. It remains in place if you become incapacitated.
    b. It allows the person you select to make financial decisions on your behalf.
    c. It cannot be changed.
    d. No one else can monitor the actions of your designated POA.

3. **If you receive a call or an email from someone claiming to be in trouble and in need of emergency funds, what should you do? Select all that apply.**
    a. Call the individual at a known home or cell phone number to verify that the need is legitimate.
    b. Immediately wire funds to the account number provided.
    c. If the call is from a hospital or law enforcement agency, look up the number of the institution and call the number you find.
    d. Hang up immediately.

4. **Your bank will never send you an email asking you to verify your account number or any other identifying information.**
    a. True
    b. False

5. Where can you check a financial adviser's background?

    a. FINRA BrokerCheck

    b. Social Security Administration

    c. State Securities Regulator

    d. Federal Trade Commission

6. Which forms of identification should you have readily available in case of emergency?

    a. Driver's License

    b. Insurance Card

    c. Social Security Card

    d. Passport

    e. Birth Certificate

7. What can you do to prepare financially for a disaster?

    a. Set up automatic bill payments.

    b. Know where to find important documentation in an emergency.

    c. Review insurance information regularly to ensure you have adequate coverage.

    d. All of the above.

8. What practices should you avoid in selecting someone to repair your roof?

    a. Getting three bids in writing from local established contractors.

    b. Using contractors who come to your door and tell you they are working for a neighbor.

    c. Asking if the contractor has the required licenses and getting license numbers.

    d. Paying in advance.

9. Match these items with the best place to keep them:

Birth certificate	Emergency evacuation bag
Medical care directives	Safe-deposit box
Passport	Fireproof safe
Important contracts	Fireproof safe
Items you may need in an emergency	Safe-deposit box

What Do You Know? – Money Smart for Older Adults

Instructor: _____ Date: _____

This form will allow you and the instructors to see what you know about protecting your finances both before and after the training. Read each statement below. Please circle the number that shows how much you agree with each statement.

I am better able to:	Before the Training				After the Training			
	Strongly Disagree	Disagree	Agree	Strongly Agree	Strongly Disagree	Disagree	Agree	Strongly Agree
1. Recognize and reduce the risk of elder financial exploitation.	1	2	3	4	1	2	3	4
2. Guard against identity theft.	1	2	3	4	1	2	3	4
3. Plan for unexpected loss of the ability to manage my finances.	1	2	3	4	1	2	3	4
4. Prepare financially for disasters.	1	2	3	4	1	2	3	4
5. Find other helpful resources for managing my money.	1	2	3	4	1	2	3	4

Evaluation Form

This evaluation will enable you to assess your observations of the *Money Smart for Older Adults* module. Please indicate the degree to which you agree with each statement by circling the appropriate number.

	Strongly Disagree	Disagree	Neutral	Agree	Strongly Agree

1. Overall, I felt the module was:
    [ ] Excellent
    [ ] Very Good
    [ ] Good
    [ ] Fair
    [ ] Poor					

2. I achieved the training objectives.	1	2	3	4	5
3. The instructions were clear and easy to follow.	1	2	3	4	5
4. The slides were clear.	1	2	3	4	5
5. The slides enhanced my learning.	1	2	3	4	5
6. The time allocation was correct for this module.	1	2	3	4	5
7. The module included sufficient examples and exercises so that I will be able to apply these new skills.	1	2	3	4	5
8. The instructor was knowledgeable and well-prepared.	1	2	3	4	5
9. The worksheets are valuable.	1	2	3	4	5
10. I will use the worksheets again.	1	2	3	4	5
11. The participants had ample opportunity to exchange experiences and ideas.	1	2	3	4	5
	None				Advanced
12. My knowledge/skill level of the subject matter before taking the module.	1	2	3	4	5
13. My knowledge/skill level of the subject matter upon completion of the module.	1	2	3	4	5

14.Name of Instructor: Instructor Rating: Please use the response scale and circle the appropriate number.	Response Scale: 5 Excellent 4 Very Good 3 Good 2 Fair 1 Poor				
Objectives were clear & attainable	1	2	3	4	5
Made the subject understandable	1	2	3	4	5
Encouraged questions	1	2	3	4	5
Had technical knowledge	1	2	3	4	5

What was the most useful part of the training?

_____

_____

_____

_____

What was the least useful part of the training and how could it be improved?

_____

_____

_____

_____

Glossary

Adult Protective Services (APS): A [state or local] agency that investigates abuse, neglect or exploitation of older adults or younger adults who have disabilities.

Affinity Fraud: A type of fraud that targets members of an identifiable group, such as a religious organization, ethnic group, older adults, or professional groups.

Agent: A person to whom you grant authority to act in your place.

Annuity: A type of investment offered by insurance companies, or by other financial institutions acting on behalf of insurance companies. Annuities allow your money to grow tax-deferred until you withdraw it. The insurer agrees to make periodic payments to you for a set period of time. Annuities are complex investments with a variety of structures. They are not appropriate for many people in or near retirement.

Variable Annuity: An insurance contract that invests your premium in various mutual fund-like investments.

Direct Deposit: An electronic method for transferring and depositing money directly into your account.

Direct Express Debit Card: A debit card that allows you to access your federal benefits without a bank account. Your federal benefits payment is deposited to your Direct Express® card account on your payment day. You can use the card to make purchases, pay bills or get cash.

Elder Financial Exploitation: An act of using an older adult's money or assets contrary to his or her wishes, needs, or best interests for the abuser's personal gain.

Electronic Transfer Account (ETA): A low-cost account that allows recipients to receive their federal payments electronically.

Fiduciary: A person who manages the assets for the benefit of another person rather than for his or her own profit.

Federal Deposit Insurance Corporation (FDIC) Deposit Insurance: Insurance that protects your money if the bank fails. However, FDIC does not insure non-deposit investment products, including: stocks, bonds, mutual funds, and annuities.

Fraud: A type of illegal act involving the obtaining of something of value through willful misrepresentation.

Grandparent Scam: A scam whereby a caller pretends to be a relative in need of immediate funds to deal with an emergency. The caller may also represent themselves as a hospital employee, law enforcement officer, or attorney.

Identity Theft: A fraud committed or attempted using the identifying information of another person without authority.

Older Adult: Someone age 62 or older.

Older Americans Act: Legislation initially passed in 1965, established authority for grants to States for community planning and social services, research and development projects, and personnel training in the field of aging. It established the Administration on Aging (AoA) to administer the newly created grant programs. Today it authorizes a wide array of service programs through a national network of 56 State agencies on aging, 629 area agencies on aging, nearly 20,000 service providers, 244 Tribal organizations, and 2 Native Hawaiian organizations representing 400 Tribes.

Pharming: When criminals seek to obtain personal or private information by making fake websites appear legitimate.

Phishing: When criminals send out unsolicited emails that appear to be from a legitimate source in an attempt to trick you into divulging personal information.

Ponzi Scheme: Also called a "pyramid" scheme, the scam artists promise high returns and use the money of some investors to pay off other investors.

Power of Attorney: A power of attorney (POA) is a legal document that allows someone to act on your behalf.

Durable Power of Attorney: A power of attorney (POA) that remains in effect even if you become incompetent.

Privacy Notices: These notices explain how the company handles and shares your personal financial information. You will usually receive a privacy notice when you open an account or become a customer of a financial company, once a year after opening an account, and any time the financial company changes its privacy policy.

Promissory Note: A promissory note is a form of debt – similar to a loan or an IOU – that a company may issue to raise money.

Reverse Mortgage: A special type of loan that allows homeowners age 62 and older to borrow against the equity in their homes.

Revocable Trust Account: A deposit account held as a payable on death (POD) or in trust for (ITF) account, or one that is established in the name of a formal revocable trust (also known as a living or family trust account).

Scam: A confidence trick, confidence game, or con for short, is an attempt to intentionally mislead a person or persons usually with the goal of financial or other gain.

Spam: Unsolicited commercial email (UCE)

Surrender Charge: A fee you incur when you sell, or cancel, certain types of investments or annuity policies.

For Further Information

Consumer Financial Protection Bureau (CFPB)

www.consumerfinance.gov

1-855-411-CFPB (2372)

The Dodd-Frank Wall Street Reform and Consumer Protection Act of 2010 (Dodd-Frank Act) created the Consumer Financial Protection Bureau to make markets for consumer financial products and services work for Americans. The Bureau works to fulfill this mission by making rules more effective, by consistently and fairly enforcing those rules, and by empowering consumers to take more control over their economic lives.

The Office for Older Americans is a special office within the CFPB that is dedicated to helping Americans age 62 and older make sound financial decisions.

The Consumer Financial Protection Bureau (CFPB) offers several resources:

- Print brochures on topics such as reverse mortgages, at http://promotions.usa.gov/cfpbpubs.html
- An online resource called *ASK CFPB*, which contains authoritative, unbiased, understandable answers to commonly-asked consumer questions with a special section for older Americans, at http://www.consumerfinance.gov/askcfpb/
- A consumer complaint line for financial products including mortgages, car loans, consumer loans, bank accounts and services, student loans and credit reporting. Complaints can be filed online at www.consumerfinance.gov/complaint/ or by calling 1-855-411-CFPB (2372)

Federal Deposit Insurance Corporation (FDIC)

www.fdic.gov/consumers

Division of Depositor & Consumer Protection

2345 Grand Boulevard, Suite 1200

Kansas City, Missouri 64108

1-877-ASK-FDIC (275-3342)

Email: consumeralerts@fdic.gov

Visit the FDIC's website for additional information and resources on consumer issues. Additional modules of the Money Smart financial education program are available online as computer based instruction. Enter *Money Smart* in the search field. The quarterly *FDIC Consumer News* provides practical hints and guidance on how to become a smarter, safer user of financial services. Also, the FDIC's Consumer Response Center is responsible for:

- Investigating all types of consumer complaints about FDIC-supervised institutions
- Responding to consumer inquiries about consumer laws and regulations and banking practices

Consumers should note that while the FDIC is responsible for insuring deposits in FDIC insured institutions, the bank itself may be chartered or supervised by other agencies (such as the Office of the Comptroller of the Currency or the Federal Reserve). To determine which regulator has jurisdiction over a particular banking institution, so you can submit a complaint to the correct agency, you can call the FDIC toll-free at 1-877-ASK-FDIC (1-877-275-3342). For consumer protection issues, you can also contact the CFPB.

Federal Trade Commission

www.ftc.gov

1-877-FTC-HELP (382-4357)

www.ftc.gov/idtheft

1/877-IDTHEFT (438-4338)

The Federal Trade Commission (FTC) website offers practical information on a variety of consumer topics. Two brochures on identity theft are available online or in print: *Taking Charge: What to do if Your Identity is Stolen* and *Identity Theft: What to Know, What to do*. The FTC also provides guidance and information on how to select a contractor: *Home Sweet Home Improvement*.

Elder Care Locator

www.eldercare.gov

1-800-677-1116

The Eldercare Locator, a public service of the Administration on Aging, U.S. Department of Health and Human Services, is a nationwide service that connects older adults and their caregivers with information on senior services. You can search for services by location or by topic.

Medicare

www.medicare.gov

1-800-MEDICARE (1-800-633-4227)

The official U.S. Government site for Medicare allows you to search for physicians and other health care providers that are enrolled in Medicare.

U.S. Department of Veterans Affairs

www.va.gov

1-800-827-1000

Look under *Veterans Services* for an online booklet describing the benefits that may be available. To find a list of accredited representatives, agents, and attorneys who can assist you in filing for benefits, visit www.va.gov/ogc/apps/accreditation/index.asp.

National Center on Elder Abuse

http://ncea.aoa.gov/

The Administration on Aging sponsored website provides resources on elder abuse prevention, including information on reporting a suspected case of elder abuse.

National Association of Area Agencies on Aging (n4a)

www.n4a.org

This umbrella organization supports a national network of more than 600 area agencies on aging and nearly 250 Title VI Native American aging programs through advocacy, training, publications, and technical assistance. It administers the Eldercare Locator.

Financial Industry Regulatory Authority

www.finra.org

1-800 289-9999 (BrokerCheck Hotline)

Find out about the broker's background via the (FINRA) BrokerCheck. Or call the FINRA BrokerCheck Hotline. Find out more about the use of senior designations or certifications at http://www.finra.org/Investors/ToolsCalculators/BrokerCheck/

OnGuardOnline.gov

www.onguardonline.gov

OnGuardOnline.gov is the federal government's website to help you be safe, secure and responsible online. The FTC manages the site in partnership with 16 other federal agencies. Its resources include information on phishing available at http://onguardonline.gov/articles/0003-phishing.

Report Financial Exploitation

If someone is in immediate danger, dial 911 or your local police department.

Adult Protective Services

Telephone numbers vary by location

Visit www.eldercare.gov

or call for contact information for your area:

1-800-677-1116

A [state or local] government agency, generally a part of your county or state department of social services, that investigates abuse, neglect or exploitation of older adults, or younger adults who have disabilities.

Federal Trade Commission

www.ftc.gov/idtheft

1/877-IDTHEFT (438-4338)

The FTC online toolkit includes a detailed guide for protecting your information, with instructions and sample letters to help identity theft victims – *Taking Charge: What to Do If Your Identity Is Stolen.* An online complaint form is available directly at www.ftccomplaintassistant.gov.

Legal advice or representation. How can I find an attorney who specializes in elder law issues?

Federally funded legal assistance programs for people 60 and older (known as Title IIIB legal services programs) can provide legal assistance on issues such as income security, health care, long-term care, nutrition, housing, utilities, protective services, defense of guardianship, abuse, neglect, and age discrimination. Legal assistance is targeted towards older individuals in social and economic need. Each program has its own priorities and eligibility guidelines regarding case acceptance and areas of representation.

Your senior legal aid program may be located at your local legal services program. You can also find out about your local legal assistance programs by contacting your area agency on aging or www.eldercarelocator.gov. If you need a private attorney to assist you with making a power of attorney, trust, will or other advance planning tool, contact the lawyer referral service of your state bar association.

Senior Medicare Patrol (SMP)

www.smpresource.org

1-877-808-2468

The SMP programs, also known as Senior Medicare Patrol programs, help Medicare and Medicaid beneficiaries avoid, detect, and prevent health care fraud. SMPs nationwide recruit and teach nearly 5,700 volunteers every year to help in this effort. Most SMP volunteers are both retired and Medicare beneficiaries and thus well-positioned to assist you. Visit the website above or call for more information or to get contact information for your state SMP.

Social Security Administration

www.ssa.gov

Toll free customer service at 1-800-772-1213. Deaf or hearing-impaired individuals can call Social Security's TTY number at 1-800-325-0778.